For

NEW ENGLAND NOTABLES

Compiled by
Lynton C. and Joan Wiener

PETER PAUPER PRESS, INC.
WHITE PLAINS, NEW YORK

For our grandchildren:
Jesse, Elizabeth, Molly,
and Jake

Copyright © 1993
Peter Pauper Press, Inc.
202 Mamaroneck Avenue
White Plains, NY 10601
All rights reserved
ISBN 0-88088-766-4
Printed in Hong Kong
7 6 5 4 3 2 1

NEW ENGLAND NOTABLES

Leverett Saltonstall, a former Massachusetts Senator, once observed: *The real New England Yankee is the person who takes the midnight train home from New York.*

Henry David Thoreau heard a *different drummer* and *went to the woods*. And

Ruth Gordon said that *if I don't make it today, I'll come in tomorrow.*

New Englanders from Maine to Connecticut are (and have always been) nothing if not articulate. This sampler of succinct quotations is the proof, and is set forth for your enjoyment.

The Editors

* * * * *

The birthplace of each New Englander quoted is noted below the name. Where no birthplace appears, it is believed that the person quoted was not New England born.

A New England con-
science doesn't keep you
from doing anything; it just
keeps you from enjoying it.

LA ROCHEFOUCAULD

Sometimes I wonder if men and women really suit each other. Perhaps they should live next door and just visit now and then.

KATHARINE HEPBURN,
Hartford, CT

*W*ho do I think I am—
everybody?

LEONARD BERNSTEIN,
Lawrence, MA

*I*t took me fifteen years to discover I had no talent for writing, but I couldn't give it up because by that time I was too famous.

ROBERT BENCHLEY,
Worcester, MA

NEW ENGLAND NOTABLES

A celebrity is a person who works hard all his life to become well known, and then wears dark glasses to avoid being recognized.

FRED ALLEN,
Boston, MA

*N*ew England has a harsh climate, a barren soil, a rough and stormy coast, and yet we love it, even with a love passing that of dwellers in more favored regions.

HENRY CABOT LODGE,
Boston, MA

NEW ENGLAND NOTABLES

*T*he courage of New
England is the courage of
conscience.

DANIEL WEBSTER,
Salisbury, NH

NEW ENGLAND NOTABLES

You remember the very old story about a citizen of Boston who heard a Texan talking about the glories of Bowie, Davy Crockett, and all the rest, and finally said, "Haven't you heard of Paul Revere?" To which the Texan answered, "Well, he is the man who ran for help."

JOHN F. KENNEDY,
Brookline, MA

A friend told me she visited a little shop in Maine and asked the saleslady if she carried a certain commodity. "We used to stock them," she replied in a perfectly rational tone, "but we always sold out right away, so we stopped ordering them."

JOSEPH GALLAGHER

*H*e comes of the Brahmin caste of New England. This is the harmless, inoffensive, untitled aristocracy.

OLIVER WENDELL HOLMES.
Boston, MA

NEW ENGLAND NOTABLES

I moved to New England partly because it has a real literary past. The ghosts of Hawthorne and Melville still sit on those green hills. The worship of Mammon is also somewhat lessened there by the spirit of irony. I don't get hay fever in New England either.

JOHN UPDIKE

I don't want to be a doctor, and live by men's diseases; nor a minister to live by their sins; nor a lawyer to live by their quarrels. So I don't see there's anything left for me but to be an author.

NATHANIEL HAWTHORNE,
Salem, MA

*G*od works wonders now
and then: Behold! A lawyer
and an honest man!

BENJAMIN FRANKLIN,
Boston, MA

*I*t was not price nor money that could have purchased Rhode Island. Rhode Island was purchased by love.

ROGER WILLIAMS

A sup of New England's air is better than a whole draft of old England's ale.

REVEREND
FRANCIS HIGGINSON

*T*he magistrate is the servant not of his own desires, not even of the people, but of his God.

JOHN ADAMS,
Braintree, MA

*I*f perticuliar care and attention is not paid to the Laidies we are determined to foment a Rebelion, and will not hold ourselves bound by any Laws in which we have no voice, or Representation.

ABIGAIL ADAMS,
Weymouth, MA
letter to John Adams

*T*he country shall be independent, and we will be satisfied with nothing short of it.

SAMUEL ADAMS,
Boston, MA

*I*t usually takes a hundred years to make a law, and then, after it has done its work, it usually takes another hundred years to get rid of it.

HENRY WARD BEECHER,
Litchfield, CT

I would rather that the people should wonder why I wasn't President than why I am.

SALMON P. CHASE,
Cornish Township, NH

*T*here never will be complete equality until women themselves help to make laws and elect lawmakers.

SUSAN B. ANTHONY,
Adams, MA

*W*hat is life but the angle of vision? A man is measured by the angle at which he looks at objects. What is life but what a man is thinking of all day? This is his fate and his employer. Knowing is the measure of the man. By how much we know, so much we are.

RALPH WALDO EMERSON,
Boston, MA

*B*eware when the great
God lets loose a thinker on
this planet.

RALPH WALDO EMERSON,
Boston, MA

NEW ENGLAND NOTABLES

The sickness—the nausea—
  The pitiless pain—
Have ceased with the fever
  That maddened my
  brain—
With the fever called
"Living"
  That burned in my brain.

EDGAR ALLAN POE,
Boston, MA
For Annie

*M*y heart was bursting
with the anguish excited by
the cruelty and injustice
our nation was showing to
the slave, and praying God
to let me do a little and to
cause my cry for them to
be heard.

HARRIET BEECHER STOWE,
Litchfield, CT

*I*f a man does not keep
pace with his companions,
perhaps it is because he
hears a different drummer.
Let him step to the music
which he hears, however
measured or far away.

HENRY D. THOREAU,
Concord, NH
Walden

I went to the woods because I wished to live deliberately, to front only the essential facts of life, and see if I could not learn what it had to teach, and not, when I came to die, discover that I had not lived.

HENRY D. THOREAU,
Concord, NH
Walden

NEW ENGLAND NOTABLES

"Shoot, if you must, this
old gray head.
But spare your country's
flag," she said.

JOHN GREENLEAF WHITTIER,
Haverhill, MA
Barbara Frietchie

*W*e are swallowed up in schemes for gain and engrossed with contrivances for bodily enjoyments, as if this particle of dust were immortal—as if the soul needed no aliment, and the mind no raiment.

HENRY WADSWORTH
LONGFELLOW,
Portland, ME

NEW ENGLAND NOTABLES

*B*eneath this soil a
Yankee lies,
    A Yankee very crankee.
Move not his bones or he'll
turn stones,
    And leap to life to
    spank 'ee.

HORATIO ALGER,
Revere, MA

Sixty years ago I knew everything; now I know nothing; education is a progressive discovery of our own ignorance.

WILL DURANT,
Boston, MA

*A*n activity which does not have worth enough to be carried on for its own sake cannot be very effective as preparation for something else.

JOHN DEWEY,
Burlington, VT

NEW ENGLAND NOTABLES

Go West, young man, go West.

HORACE GREELEY,
Amherst, NH

I have always been driven by some distant music—a battle hymn no doubt—for I have been at war from the beginning. I've never looked back before, I've never had the time and it has always seemed so dangerous.

BETTE DAVIS,
Lowell, MA

*N*obody deserves this much money—certainly not an actor.

JACK LEMMON,
Newton Center, MA

After years of dealing with their tantrums and their egos, I have come to one conclusion: actors are children.

DAVID SUSSKIND,
Brookline, MA

*F*orgive yourself for the past so that you can love yourself now and tomorrow.

LINDA EVANS,
Hartford, CT

I'm having trouble
managing the mansion.
What I need is a wife.

ELLA T. GRASSO,
Windsor Locks, CT
Governor of Connecticut

NEW ENGLAND NOTABLES

*F*ears of nuclear war were largely confined to children of liberal, affluent parents, themselves concerned about nuclear war.

ROBERT COLES,
Milton, MA

*R*emember, my son, that any man who is a bear on the future of this country will go broke.

J. PIERPONT MORGAN,
Hartford, CT

NEW ENGLAND NOTABLES

*W*hat hath God wrought!

SAMUEL F. B. MORSE,
Charlestown, MA
first Morse Code transmission

I am the inferior of any man whose rights I trample underfoot.

HORACE GREELEY,
Amherst, NH

O Prejudice.... You enter into the little boy of a New England town and make him stand and gape with the same horror at [the] man going into a Catholic church as the man going into a saloon.

CHARLES IVES,
Danbury, CT

*I*n a world where there is so much to be done, I felt strongly impressed that there must be something for me to do.

DOROTHEA DIX,
Hampden, ME

*B*eware of Greeks bearing gifts, colored men looking for loans, and whites who understand the Negro.

ADAM CLAYTON POWELL,
New Haven, CT

*I*t is wise statesmanship which suggests that in time of peace we must prepare for war, and it is no less a wise benevolence that makes preparation in the hour of peace for assuaging the ills that are sure to accompany war.

CLARA BARTON,
North Oxford, MA

Goodwill is the one and
only asset that competition
cannot undersell nor
destroy.

MARSHALL FIELD,
Conway, MA

*T*here's a sucker born
every minute.

P. T. BARNUM,
Bethel, CT

NEW ENGLAND NOTABLES

*V*ermont is my birthright. People there are happy and content. They belong to themselves, live within their income, and fear no man.

CALVIN COOLIDGE,
Plymouth, VT

*T*he chief problem of the
lower-income farmers is
poverty.

NELSON ROCKEFELLER,
Bar Harbor, ME

*T*his organization [the UN] is created to prevent you from going to hell. It isn't created to take you to heaven.

HENRY CABOT LODGE,
Boston, MA

*T*he three ages of man:
youth, middle age, and
"You're looking wonderful!"

FRANCIS CARDINAL
SPELLMAN,
Whitman, MA

I looked on child rearing not only as a work of love and duty but as a profession that was fully as interesting and challenging as any honorable profession in the world and one that demanded the best that I could bring to it.

ROSE FITZGERALD
KENNEDY,
Boston, MA

NEW ENGLAND NOTABLES

I hate the theater. That whole thing about the theater being sacred is ridiculous. It's full of boring, unimaginative, third-rate people. Every good actor I know has moved to Hollywood.

ESTELLE PARSONS,
Lynn, MA

*B*eing given good
material is like being
assigned to bake a cake
and having the batter
made for you.

ROSALIND RUSSELL,
Waterbury, CT

NEW ENGLAND NOTABLES

I've missed all the corny stuff. I've missed smelling the flowers. . . . I'm always on the phone saying, "I'll make this fast." Just once I'd like to get on the phone and say, "Let's make it slow. I have no place to go."

BARBARA WALTERS,
Boston, MA

*W*e make up horrors to help us cope with the real ones.

STEPHEN KING,
Portland, ME

A man that does not know how to be angry does not know how to be good.

HENRY WARD BEECHER,
Litchfield, CT

*[I*n architecture] form
follows function.

LOUIS HENRI SULLIVAN,
Boston, MA

Civilization begins with order, grows with liberty, and dies with chaos.

WILL DURANT,
Boston, MA

*W*hatever you do, kid--
always serve it with a little
dressing.

GEORGE M. COHAN,
Providence, RI
to Spencer Tracy

*I*f I don't make it today,
I'll come in tomorrow.

RUTH GORDON,
Wollaston, MA

Another picture, I imagine.
Or, perhaps, another world.

CECIL B. DE MILLE,
Ashfield, MA
one week before his death,
about his plans

NEW ENGLAND NOTABLES

You know what I'm going
to have on my grave stone?
"She did it the hard way."

BETTE DAVIS,
Lowell, MA

NEW ENGLAND NOTABLES

*I*n Maine we have a
saying that there's no point
in speaking unless you can
improve on silence.

EDMUND MUSKIE,
Rumford, ME